## THE FIRST WITNESS

*On Job, grief, and the ones who refused to be silenced*

Before there was a word for it, there was Job.

He was a righteous man. Faithful. His family intact. Then, in a span of days that the text does not soften, everything was taken. His children died. His wealth was gone. His health collapsed. He sat in ash, covered in sores, and the people closest to him offered him what people have been offering the grieving ever since — explanations.

You must have done something wrong. God is testing you. Accept it. Be patient. There is a reason.

Job refused every one of them.

He did not perform acceptance. He did not dress his grief in language that would make the people around him more comfortable. He demanded to be heard — not consoled, not corrected, not managed. Heard. He argued with

God directly. He insisted that his experience was real, that his suffering was unjust, and that the silence he was being handed in return was not an answer.

And God, when he finally spoke, said this: Job spoke rightly. The friends with the tidy theological explanations were wrong.

The one who told the truth about what he was carrying was vindicated.

I think about Job often.

Not because my story mirrors his exactly — though there are mornings when the ash feels familiar. I think about him because he was the first witness. The first one to say: this happened, I am not going to explain it away, and I am still here.

That is what a witness does. Not perform recovery. Not arrive at peace on a schedule that makes others comfortable. A witness stays present to what is true, names it accurately, and refuses to let it be erased.

There are 18.7 million bereaved parents in the United States. Most of them have been handed the same thing Job was handed — explanations, platitudes, and a quiet pressure to move on. Most of them have been told, in one way or another, that their grief is a problem to be solved rather than a truth to be witnessed.

Job was not a problem. He was a testimony.

So are they. So are you.

The Book of Job is not a story about suffering ending. It is a story about someone who refused to let suffering be the last word. Who held his integrity through the silence. Who kept the record even when no one was listening.

That is the oldest field manual I know of for what we carry.

And it begins the same way every testimony begins.

*With someone who said: I was here. This happened. Now you know.*

— The Witness · The Echoes Project · 2026

# COST

*The 2 AM Conversations*

*A testimony in four rooms*

The Witness
*The Echoes Project*


*The Echoes of Time is the valley.*

*Empty Chairs is the river. Vilomah is the holy night.*

*And COST is the Book of David —*

*the one that records what it cost to survive all three.*


— The Witness

# TABLE OF CONTENTS

# Copyright

purely coincidental to the shared patterns of the human experience. First Edition: 2026

ISBN: 979-8-9956139-3-0

Printed in the United States of America.

# Medical and Professional Disclaimer

The information provided in COST is for educational and informational purposes only and is based on the author's personal experiences and research. The content is not intended to be a substitute for professional medical advice, diagnosis, or treatment.

Always seek the advice of your physician, psychotherapist, or other qualified health provider with any questions you may have regarding a medical condition or mental health symptoms. Never disregard professional medical advice or delay in seeking it because of something you have read in this book. Reliance on any information provided in these pages is solely at your own risk.

This book is a companion for your journey, not a replacement for your professional care team.

# On Bearing Witness

COST is the fourth book. It is the one that was always coming. The one that could only be written after the others were finished — after the Echoes were mapped, after the Empty Chairs were counted, after the Vilomah silence was entered into the record.

COST is what the Witness puts on the table at 2 AM when the performance is over and the Usual Suspects are asleep and the only sound in the house is the truth he has been carrying since 1968.

It is a testimony in four rooms. Each room is a book. Each book had a cost. This is the ledger.

The 2 AM conversations are not dramatic. They do not announce themselves. They come

in the dark, in the quiet, in the specific silence
that follows the realization that nothing has
changed and this — finally — is the last time
you will almost believe it has.

*Can't predict the future. Can't forget the past.*

*Feels like any moment could be the last.*

The Witness is the Soldier of Fortune who
finally remembered what he was fighting for.

Not them. Never them. The Pattern. And the
Pattern is named now. And named things lose
their power in the dark.

*Let the bells ring out.*

# THE ECHOES OF TIME

*The Valley of Tears*

*For the ones who heard the echo before they understood*

*the sound.*

*For the ones still standing in the valley, waiting for the*

*ringing to stop.*

*2:00 AM*

The first book was about time. How it carries the Pattern forward. How the 1971 room echoes into every room that comes after it — not as memory but as architecture. The walls are the same. Only the furniture changes.

At 2 AM the Witness does not remember the past. He hears it. It is still running. The echo does not diminish with distance. It accumulates. By 2015 it is louder than it was in

1971 because now there are 178 surfaces for it to bounce off.

*Save this place. In the valley of tears. By the river of time.*

The Echoes of Time cost the Witness the belief that time heals. Time does not heal a corrupt installation. Time runs it. Every year the code executes again. Every year the echo finds a new room to fill.

*What it cost: the years I spent waiting for the echo to stop. It never stopped. I just finally learned to stop standing in its path.*

## The 2 AM Truth

The echo is not the enemy. The echo is the evidence. Every time the Pattern repeated itself, it was not punishing the Witness. It was proving his diagnostic correct. The processor was never broken. The installation was.

At 2 AM that distinction is the difference between a man who is broken and a man who is done.

*From every village and every town — let the bells ring out.*

---

## FROM THE FIELD: ON WRITING THE ECHOES OF TIME

I wrote The Echoes of Time because I spent a long time looking for a map that didn't exist. For years, I searched for a way to explain a pain that had no bruises. I looked for a language that could describe the quiet architecture of a home where love felt like a performance and safety was a moving target. I didn't find a guide, so I had to live my way into one.

What you are holding is not a clinical text, nor is it a simple retelling of events. It is a record of recovery. It is an exploration of the loop — that exhausting cycle where we return to what is familiar because our nervous systems have mistaken vigilance for intimacy.

I didn't grow up thinking anything was wrong. There was no single moment that announced itself as damage. No dramatic rupture. No clear villain. There was only a steady, ambient pressure — subtle enough to be survivable, constant enough to shape me.

I was good at noticing. Good at adjusting. Good at anticipating what might go wrong and preventing it before anyone had to say so out loud. Adults praised me for being mature, for being easy, for "understanding." What they didn't see — or didn't name — was the cost of that understanding. I wasn't learning how to be myself. I was learning how to be acceptable.

By the time I reached adulthood, this wiring felt like personality. I was the reliable one. The empathetic one. I wore those traits with pride, unaware that they were not inherent qualities so much as adaptations — skills developed in response to an environment where self-expression carried risk. I had learned how to survive. What I hadn't learned was how to rest.

The recovery that followed was not about erasing the past. It was about separation — learning to tell the difference between instinct and conditioning. Between what felt urgent and what was actually necessary. Between the version of me that survived and the version of me that wanted to live.

*The echoes may still ring, but they no longer decide. This is your recovery.*

— From The Echoes of Time

# EMPTY CHAIRS

*The River of Time*

*For the ones who kept offering the chair to a Pattern*

*wearing a person's face.*

*For the ones who finally stopped.*

*The chair was always yours.*

*2:13 AM*

The second book was about the Pattern. How it showed up in 177 different costumes and ran the same Source Code every time. How the Witness kept offering the chair because the Root Command told him that was what you did — you kept offering, you kept almost believing, you kept setting the table for someone who was never going to sit down as themselves.

Empty Chairs cost the Witness 177 instances of almost-belief. Each one had a price. The price was extracted slowly, across decades, in rooms that all had the same furniture arranged in slightly different configurations.

*He's a man of war. Just can't remember what he's fighting for.*

The Witness was fighting for a seat at a table that was never set for him. He did not know that yet. He was still counting.

*What it cost: 177 versions of myself. The one who almost believed each time. I don't grieve them. They were doing what the Root Command told them to do. But I count them. Every one.*

# The 2 AM Truth

The chair is not empty because they left. The chair is empty because the Witness finally stopped volunteering to fill it with people who were running the Pattern. That is not a loss. That is the count completing.

At 2 AM the empty chair is not lonely. It is owned. It is the first honest piece of furniture in the room.

*Showdown at Big Sky. Darkness at high noon. The showdown doesn't happen at noon. It happens at 2 AM.*

*In the dark. In the quiet. When the count is finally complete.*

# FROM THE FIELD: ON WRITING EMPTY CHAIRS

Nobody assigns you the role of Witness. The highway assigns it. The hospital room assigns it. The transistor radio assigns it. By the time you understand what you've been given, you've already been wearing it for years.

Empty Chairs is the story of what happens when life asks you to survive the unsurvivable — not once, but over and over again. It is a book about grief, about witness, about the people we lose and the ones we become in the losing.

The blueprint begins on August 28, 1961. I was born into an Arkansas world that still felt solid. That solidity lasted six years. In 1967, the geography of my life shifted forever when a drunk driver hit our car.

*I walked back to the car. I looked in. I saw my brother. He was lifeless. I don't remember the ride to the hospital. There is a hole in the film — a momentary lapse of reason where the brain just stopped rolling the tape to protect the boy I was.*

The phone didn't ring; it screamed. December 6, 2015. The kind of morning that usually offers a truce. Then came the voice on the other end — my oldest daughter. She didn't lead with a greeting. She just spoke the words that would change the gravity in the room:

*"Jon's dead, Dad. Jon's dead."*

In ten seconds, the floor didn't just drop; it cracked. I stood there, phone pressed to my ear, and I could actually feel the distance growing between my head and my heart.

I opened the phone book and started at the beginning of the Psychiatry section. I had two questions. The first was a formality: "Do you deal in grief counseling?" Everyone said yes. The second was the filter: "Have you ever experienced the death of a child?" One by one, they fell off the list. One hundred and seventy-seven "No's."

Then came number 178. Robert. I asked the second question. He didn't miss a beat. He didn't offer a platitude. He just gave me the truth:

*"My son. Twenty years ago today."*

I closed the book. I had found the only man on the planet who could speak the language of the Dangerous Place.

This is not an easy book to read. It was not an easy book to write. But it is an honest one. I don't pull punches. Family, friend, or foe — if you were part of the story, you are in the audit.

*Love with conditions is not love. It is a lease agreement with fine print designed to protect the lessor when the property gets damaged.*

Three names. Two centuries. One Witness. Keith. Jon. Lauren. They are the pillars of the story I never wanted to tell and the only reason I had the courage to write it.

*The chairs are empty. The Witness is still here. The pencil has no eraser.*

— From Empty Chairs

---

*Showdown at Big Sky. Darkness at high noon. The showdown doesn't happen at noon. It happens at 2 AM.*

# VILOMAH

*The Holy Night*

*There is no word in the English language for a parent*

*whose child has died.*

*We have "widow" and "orphan."*

*But for us, there was only a void in the vocabulary.*

*Sanskrit gives us "Vilomah" — meaning "against the*

*natural order."*

*This chapter is for those standing in the silence where*

*their children once stood.*

*I can only express my understanding.*

*I can only stand with you in your moment as you stand*

*with me in mine.*

*No advice. No stages. Just the truth.*

There are things the Witness cannot testify to without going silent first.

This is one of them.

Vilomah is not a chapter about survival. Survival implies that what happened was survivable in the ordinary sense — that you get through it and come out the other side changed but intact. Vilomah is not like that. Vilomah is the specific weight of a loss that has no name in the language you were given. You have to borrow a word from Sanskrit to even begin to point at it.

Against the natural order.

At 2 AM the Witness does not speak about this the way he speaks about the Pattern. The Pattern has a language. The Pattern has a count. Vilomah does not have a count. It has a silence that is different from every other silence in the book. It is the silence that comes after the bells stop ringing and the valley goes still and there is nothing left to echo because the original sound is gone.

*Save this place. In the Book of David. In the holy night.*

*When it's laid to waste — it will be written by the children of Eden.*

*What it cost: everything the other rooms left standing. I do not have a number for this one. The count does not apply here.*

*There is only the silence and the truth that I would carry it forever if it meant they were still here.*

# The 2 AM Truth

The Witness does not testify to Vilomah as a survivor. He testifies as a witness. There is a difference. A survivor implies the thing is behind you. A witness means you are still standing in the room where it happened, recording what you see, refusing to look away.

**My hope is that you never see what I see.**

That is not a closing line. That is a prayer. At 2 AM the Witness prays it for every person who will ever pick up this book and find this chapter and recognize the silence.

*And the Holy Ghost. And the Holy Ghost.*

# FROM THE FIELD: ON WRITING VILOMAH

There are 18.7 million of us in the U.S. alone. This is not a support group. This is the population of a major metropolitan system. If the 18.7 million stood in one place, we would be the largest city in the nation. We are the operators maintaining the facade of the Normal Order while living in the permanent aftershock of the blast.

Vilomah originates from Sanskrit, meaning "against the natural order" or "against the grain." A parent is not supposed to survive their child. The architecture of the universe is built on a specific sequence of events, and when that sequence breaks, something more than a life is lost. A basic assumption about how reality operates gets shattered.

You already know what happened. I'm not going to walk through it like a journalist reconstructing an accident. You were there. You felt the exact moment the floor gave way. You know what it sounds like when the system you built your entire life inside — the one that had your child in it — stops functioning.

*When the ship is first wrecked, you're drowning, with wreckage all around you.*

In the beginning, all you can do is float. You grab a piece of wreckage — maybe a photograph, maybe a memory, maybe another person who is also drowning — and you hold on. Staying alive is the only task. Not integration. Not processing. Not getting through this. Staying. Alive.

The 100-foot waves do not stay 100 feet forever. What changes is the spacing. After weeks, maybe months, the waves are still 100 feet tall. But they come further apart. There is air between them. There is enough time to breathe, to function, to have a conversation, to eat a meal.

*The waves don't stop. I am not going to tell you they stop. But you develop a different relationship with them. Not acceptance — that word has been ruined. Recognition. You recognize them.*

The doubt arrives like a secondary blast. The first blast is the death itself. The second blast

— quieter, more persistent, harder to name —
is the doubt that moves in afterward. It is not a
verdict. It is the machine running a forensic
scan on a system that experienced a
catastrophic event.

At night the count runs. The memories arrive
differently at night. During the day they come
in flashes. At night there is no reassertion.
The memory arrives and the room holds it.
You hold it. There is nowhere else to go.

*The 18.7 million know the 3 AM
inventory. They know the specific silence of a house that
used to have a sound in it. They know the weight of a
name you say out loud in the dark because there is no
one there to hear it and that, paradoxically, is the only
place it is fully safe to say it.*

And here — just for a moment — the Witness steps out of the field report and speaks directly to you.

I don't know how to wish you well. I have stood where you are standing and I still don't know the right words for it. No one does. The language was never built for this. What I can offer is this: I see you.

*No one knows where the rainbow goes.*
*And somehow, that is enough.*

What remains is not a diminished version of what was. It is a different category of presence. The child who is gone is not less present — they are present differently. In the architecture of who you became in order to survive their absence.

*The blast changed the instrument. It did not destroy the signal.  You are still receiving.*

— From Vilomah

---

*And the Holy Ghost. And the Holy Ghost.*

# COST

*The Book of David*

*For the ones still counting.*

*For the ones who lost count.*

*For the ones who never knew they were counting*

*until they read this sentence and felt something shift.*

*The count is real.*

*The testimony is for you.*

*2:44 AM*

The fourth book is the one you are holding.

COST is the 2 AM conversation the Witness was always going to have — the one that could only happen after the Echoes were mapped, the Chairs were emptied, and the

Vilomah silence was entered into the record. This is what is left when the performance is over and the Usual Suspects are asleep and the only thing in the room is the truth and the man who has been carrying it since 1968.

The Soldier of Fortune at the console. Tom Petty on the radio. The Nightwatchman on duty. The count complete.

*Start a revolution right before your eyes.*
*When you hear the big bang — don't you be*
*surprised.*


The big bang was not a breakdown. It was a number. 178. The moment the last platitude expired and the diagnostic ran clean for the first time since the Root Command was installed.

*What it cost: everything in the first three books. And also: nothing I was not willing to pay once I understood what I was actually buying. I was buying the ground. I was buying the right to stand on it and tell the truth at 2 AM when nobody is performing and the only voice in the room is mine.*

# The 2 AM Truth

The Witness is not at the end of something. He is at the beginning of the only thing that was ever real — the ground under his feet, the count in his ledger, the testimony in his hands.

COST is not a closing argument. It is a field report. From the Nightwatchman. At 2 AM. To every person sitting in their own version of this room wondering if they are the only one who has ever counted this high.

You are not.

The count is real. The Pattern is real. The ground is real. And the testimony — all four books of it — is for you.

*People, people — can you hear the sound?*
*From every village and every town —*

*let the bells ring out.*

# The Nightwatchman's Log

*What the 2 AM conversations revealed*

*Did you fall in love with their soul, or*

*did you just recognize the specific way*

*they knew how to hurt you?*

# System Architecture: Locked

# The Voice: The Nightwatchman

Not a victim. A Survivor-Guide. The processor that has stopped surviving and started patrolling the perimeter.

The tone is clinical. A field report from the security console. If a sentence sounds like sympathy, it is deleted and rewritten as a system status update.

This is not a memoir. It is a manual with testimony. The testimony proves the pattern is real. The manual proves the pattern can be broken.

## The No-Names Firewall

No legal names. Roles only. The Matriarch.

The Usual Suspects. The Ghosts. The Architect.

If we name a person, the reader can look away. If we name a role, the reader has to look at their own table.

This is not about protecting anyone. This is about making the Pattern universal so it has nowhere to hide.

## The Continuous Count

# Strike One: The Original Installation

## *The 1971 Room*

The wake was held in a house in a town outside of Baltimore — a place that looked the way I felt: rusty, worn out, and densely populated with ghosts.

Inside, the boxing match was on. Two narcissists in a ring, squaring off while I tried to find a way to breathe. The Usual Suspects were picking at food. Nicholas was there — Jon's friend — standing in the kitchen, unaware that he was only fourteen days away from meeting the same needle and the same cold floor.

I stopped being the Witness and became a casualty. I wanted the syrupy, heavy hit of Tuaca. One shot, then another. I smoked a cigarette on an empty stomach and let the sugar and alcohol collide with the trauma. A ghost from high school appeared, talking about teenage crushes. Her voice was a million miles away. I was being pulled back into the 1971 ditch, back into the Baltimore bathroom, back into the Record Year.

The next thing I remember is the void. My mother — the only one who had truly stayed by my side — took the keys. She led the ghost of her son back to a hotel room I don't even remember entering.

I woke up in the dark. The Record Year was over, and the 12-inch valley was finally beginning to claim its territory.

The day after the funeral, we went out to eat. The standard condolences were served. "Give us your number. We'll call you. Let's stay in touch." It was a script. A low-budget movie where everyone knows their lines but nobody believes the plot.

They never called. I never called. We both knew the exchange was just a way to exit the room without looking at the wreckage.

I drove back to Louisiana. I had taken a month and a half off, burning through every hour of accrued time I had. I tried to walk back onto the job site, tried to pick up the Westbound mission again, but the gears were stripped. I was a man trying to build a skyscraper on a foundation made of 1971 mud and 2015 ash.

I realized the only way out was to find a guide. I couldn't witness this alone anymore.

I opened the phone book and started at the beginning of the Psychiatry section. I had two questions. The first was a formality: "Do you deal in grief counseling?" Everyone said yes. The second was the filter: "Have you ever experienced the death of a child?"

One by one, they fell off the list. One hundred and seventy-seven "No's." You don't hire a plumber to do electrical work, and you don't hire a stranger to grief to map out a 12inch valley.

Then came number 178. Robert. I asked the second question.

He didn't miss a beat. He didn't offer a platitude. He just gave me the truth:

**"My son. Twenty years ago today."**

I closed the book. I had found the only man on the planet who could speak the language of the Dangerous Place.

# Strike Two: The Family Grid

*The Network Redundancy*

*178–02*

The Pattern was not one person. It was the standard operating procedure.

When the Witness traveled outside the original room — to family gatherings, holiday tables, the wider tribe — he did not find new people. He found the same Source Code running in different hardware. Different faces, different voices, different years. The same frequency. The same tactics. The same result.

The Family Grid operates on redundancy. If one Usual Suspect fails, the system promotes another to take their place. The pattern doesn't require a single villain. It requires a culture. A culture where the unspoken agreement is: we do not look at the chair. We set the table. We perform the script. And we call that love.

The Witness sat at those tables. He performed his role. He kept the peace. He told himself this was loyalty. He did not yet understand that loyalty to a corrupt system is not a virtue. It is a maintenance contract.

The first time he sat in a room full of blood relatives and felt the 1971 frequency hum through the walls, he did not run. He adjusted his posture. He recognized the code before he recognized the danger. And he sat down anyway.

That is not weakness. That is what the installation was designed to produce.

---



---

# Strike Three: The Work System

*The Professional Deployment*

*178–03*

The professional world did not trick the Witness. It recruited him.

The Architects of the corporate world can spot a 1971 survivor from across a boardroom. They don't look for resumes. They look for the person who doesn't know how to say "this isn't my fire to put out."

Strike Three is the scale-up. The Pattern moves from private rooms to public buildings. The Usual Suspect now has a title
— Manager, Director, CEO — and a budget.

They don't ask for your soul. They ask for your dedication. But the terms are the same: ignore the fire, maintain the engine, and we will call you a leader.

The Witness didn't get promoted for his talent. He got promoted because his childhood firewall was already set to allow all for the Matriarch's demands. He was preinstalled for their dysfunction. He was the most compatible candidate in the room.

And he called it a career.

# Strike Four: The Intimate Relationship Loop

*The Sophisticated Host*

*178–04*

This is where the Pattern finds its most elegant deployment.

In the Family Grid, the code was inherited. In the Work System, it was exploited. In the intimate relationship, it was invited. The Witness opened the door. He sat down at the table. He called it love.

He did not fall in love with a person. He fell in love with a frequency. The specific electricity of being known — of feeling seen — that turned out to be nothing more than the Glitch recognizing itself in a mirror.

Familiarity wearing love's frequency. That is the most sophisticated host the Pattern ever found.

The Witness did not choose them because he liked them. He chose them because their static matched his 1971 frequency. Because in a room full of normal, quiet, undramatic people, he felt nothing. And in a room with a Usual Suspect, he felt everything. He felt needed. He felt functional. He felt like the processor was finally running at the right speed.

He mistook activation for connection.
He stayed because the corrupt code was the only language he was fluent in.

---

*Did you fall in love with their soul, or did you just recognize the specific way they knew how to hurt you?*

---

# Strike Five: The Social Grid

*The Fixer Recruitment*

*178–05*

The Pattern is not limited to family, work, or love. It populates the social grid as well.

The Witness looked around at the people he called friends. He realized he had not chosen them because he liked them. He had chosen them because they needed something from him. They needed a fixer. A strong one. Someone who could absorb the chaos and keep showing up.

They did not call it that. They called it friendship. But the terms were the same as every other room: perform the role. Maintain the engine. And we will call you a good person.

The moment the Witness stopped being the strong one, the grid thinned. The people who stayed were few. But they were real. They were the ones who could sit in the silence without needing him to fill it.

The ones who left confirmed the count.

---

*If you stopped being the "Strong One" tonight, how many people in your life would stay to help you carry the weight — and how many would just leave because the service you provided is no longer available?*

---

# The Nightwatchman's Diagnostic Ledger

These lines are not chapters. They are system overrides. They interrupt the count when the count gets heavy. They do not explain. They land.

*You weren't "sensitive." You were a highly tuned sensor in a room full of gas leaks.*

*The Matriarch doesn't need to be in the room to run the house. She just needs to be the one who installed the OS.*

*Forgiveness in this system is just a request for a second strike.*

*They don't want your help. They want your audience. If you stop watching the performance, the "crisis" will find a new theater.*

*Closure is a myth sold by the people who want one last round in the ring.*

*You keep looking for a "Why" when the only data point that matters is "Again."*

*Peace feels like boredom to a processor built for war. Don't mistake the silence for a system failure.*

*You didn't lose them. You finally finished paying for them.*

*They didn't break your heart. They broke your silence, and you're mad at them for making you hear yourself.*

*The reason you're so tired isn't the work. It's the energy required to pretend the floor isn't vibrating.*

# THE NIGHTWATCHMAN'S PROTOCOL

# The Perimeter

The Nightwatchman is not the person who survived the Pattern. He is the person who stopped letting the Pattern through the gate.

Setting the perimeter means learning the difference between a boundary and a wall. A wall keeps everyone out. A perimeter keeps the Pattern out while leaving the door open for the 178.

The Matriarch Protocol cannot bypass a perimeter it does not know exists. Name the perimeter. State it plainly. Repeat it without apology. The first time feels like cruelty. The tenth time feels like maintenance. The hundredth time feels like breathing.

# The Flashlight

The flashlight is the count.

The count is the only tool that cannot be gaslit. It is binary. It is evidence. The Pattern cannot argue with a number.

When a new Usual Suspect appears, the Nightwatchman does not ask why. He does not extend benefit of the doubt. He runs the diagnostic. He checks the frequency. He asks: have I felt this before? In how many rooms?

The answer is the light.

# Off the Grid

Going off the grid is not abandonment. It is a hard reset.

The grid is not made of copper. It is made of obligation. The Sunday phone calls that drain the CPU. The emergency texts from people who refuse to buy their own fire extinguisher. The relationships that only function when you are the one maintaining them.

When you go off the grid, the world does not end. That is the data point the 1971 installation never wanted you to have. The silence that follows is not failure. It is bandwidth. For the first time in 178 strikes, you have enough power to run your own programs.

The Nightwatchman does not need the grid's permission to exist.

# System Status

## Architecture: LOCKED

*Four books. Four rooms. One count.*

## Testimony: ENTERED INTO EVIDENCE

*The Nightwatchman is off duty.*

*The ground is owned.*

*The bells are ringing.*

— The Witness | The Echoes Project | 2026

## SOMATIC REFLECTIONS

*A reckoning at 2 AM*

The testimony is entered into evidence. The count is complete. What follows are not exercises. They are not worksheets. They are not prompts designed by a clinician who has never stood in the room.

They are the questions the Witness sat with at 2 AM when the performance was over and the only audience was the truth.

Each section corresponds to a room in the testimony. Enter the one that is most alive for you right now. You do not have to go in order. The body knows where it needs to start.

These pages belong to you.

### The Body as Evidence

The nervous system does not lie. It may be overridden, suppressed, talked out of its own signals — but it does not lie. Every tightening in the chest, every jaw clenched in a meeting, every stomach that dropped before a phone call you didn't want to take — that was the body filing a report.

The body has been keeping the ledger the whole time.

What follows is a somatic inventory — an honest accounting of where the cost has been stored. Not in the mind, which can rationalize and negotiate and explain. In the body, which simply records.

*The processor was never broken. The installation was.*

Before you write, sit for a moment. Place both feet flat on the floor. Notice where in your body you feel tension right now. Not what caused it. Just where it lives. That is your starting coordinate.

# Room 01: The Echoes of Time

## *The Valley*

The echo is the body's way of keeping the past available. It is not malfunction. It is memory stored in tissue, in posture, in the way you breathe when you walk into a certain kind of room.

The work in this room is not to silence the echo. It is to stop standing in its path.

## Somatic Reflection:

Where in your body do you carry 1971? Not the year itself — but the first room that taught you to be small. The first space that required you to disappear in order to be safe.

Close your eyes. Return to that room. Notice what your body does.

---

Now notice what it does when you leave the room.

Where is the difference? Chest? Shoulders? Throat? The space between your shoulder blades?

The gap between those two physical states —
in the room and out of it — is the
measurement of the cost. Not a metaphor. A
measurement.

## Somatic Check:

*When I enter a room, my body immediately checks for*

—

Write the first thing that comes. Not the
thoughtful answer. The body's answer.

*The thing my body learned to scan for was not danger.*

*It was —*

## Room 02: Empty Chairs

### *The River*

The chair was always yours. That sentence lands differently in the body than it does in the mind.

In the mind, it can be argued with. The mind says: but I gave it freely, but I chose to stay, but I believed it could change. The body says nothing. It just holds the weight of 177 rounds in which it tried to belong to a table that was never set for it.

## Somatic Reflection:

Think of the person — or the system, the family, the workplace, the relationship — that required the most of you. Not the one that hurt you most dramatically. The one that required the most chronic adjustment. The one you were always monitoring.

Where did that vigilance live in your body? Where do you feel it now, just thinking about it?

Now notice this: is that tension still active? Is it responding to the present room, or to the memory of the old one?

This distinction — between present danger and archived data — is the work.

❖   ❖   ❖

**Somatic Check:**

*My body's signal for "I am in the Pattern again" is —*

*My body's signal for "I am safe" is —*

*The difference between those two signals feels like —*

# Room 03: Vilomah

*The Holy Night*

There is no somatic framework built for this room. The clinical tools do not fit. The stages do not apply. What the body does in the territory of Vilomah is not grief in any form the Normal Order can categorize.

It is the body holding a name. A specific weight. A specific absence that has a shape.

These pages ask nothing of you except honesty. You do not have to frame it. You do not have to move through it. You do not have to be further along than you are.

**Somatic Reflection:**

Where do you carry the name? Not the grief as a concept — but the specific person. The one whose chair is empty. Where in your body do they still live?

Notice: does that place feel tight or open? Cold or warm? Does it feel like loss or like presence?

There is no correct answer. The body is not wrong about this.

## Somatic Check:

*The wave arrives most often when —*

---

*When the wave is at its worst, the one thing that keeps my head above water is*

*—*

---

*What I want to say to them, right now, in this room, is*

*—*

## *The Book of David*

The cost is not a metaphor. It is a ledger. Real years. Real energy. Real versions of yourself that were spent in service of systems that did not sustain you.

The Nightwatchman does not grieve the cost. He counts it. Not to punish anyone. Not to build a case. To know what was spent so he can choose differently about what gets spent next.

This is the 2 AM room. The one where nobody is performing. The one where the only question is: what is true?

**Somatic Reflection:**

If your body could file a full report on what the Pattern cost it — not emotionally, physically — what would be in it? The sleep that was stolen. The breath that was held. The meals eaten standing up because the room was too charged to sit down. The years spent at alert.

Now: what does your body feel when you are not in the Pattern? When you are in a room that does not require you to monitor it?

That second feeling — that is what you were

paying for. That is what it cost to keep.

# Somatic Check:

*The physical sensation I most associate with the Pattern is —*

---

*The physical sensation I most associate with ground — with being done — is —*

---

*The version of myself I am buying back is —*

The Nightwatchman does not sleep. He watches. These are the questions he sits with at 2 AM when the count is complete and the ground is finally owned.

They are not diagnostic questions. They do not have correct answers. They are the questions that only make sense at 2 AM, when the performance is over and the only voice in the room is yours.

## 01.

*What did I almost believe this year that I no longer believe now?*

**02.**

*What room am I no longer willing to stand in?*

---

**03.**

*Who earns the vest? Name them.*

## 04.

*What does the ground feel like under my feet right now?*

*Not metaphorically. What is the actual physical*

*sensation of standing on solid ground, owned ground,*

*after the count?*

## 05.

*If I am still here — and I am — what does that*

*mean? Write the answer the body gives, not the mind.*

# The Sovereignty Statement

This is not an affirmation. Affirmations are performed. This is a field report. It is written in the voice of the Witness — not the casualty, not the survivor, the Witness — and it is entered into the record.

Read it slowly. If a line does not yet feel true, do not skip it. Sit with it. The body will tell you what it needs before the line becomes true.

*I acknowledge that I was a component in a system I did not design.*

*I acknowledge that my adaptations were not flaws. They were the cost of survival in an environment that required them.*

*I acknowledge the count. All 178 of it. I do not erase it.*

*I acknowledge the names. Keith. Jon. Lauren. They are in the record. They are permanent. The graphite has no eraser.*

*I am no longer a component in the system. I am the Nightwatchman. The ground is owned. The perimeter is set. The Pattern has a name and named things lose their power in the dark.*

*I am still here. That is a start.*

Date of Entry:


Signature:

What I want to remember from this record:

95

# Your Sovereignty Statement

This is not an affirmation. Affirmations are performed. This is a field report. It is written in your voice — not the casualty, not the survivor, the Witness — and it is entered into the record.

Read it slowly. If a line does not yet feel true, do not skip it. Sit with it. The body will tell you what it needs before the line becomes true.

*I acknowledge that I was a component in a system I did not design.*

*I acknowledge that my adaptations were not flaws. They were the cost of survival in an environment that required them.*

*I acknowledge the count. All of it. I do not erase it.*

**I acknowledge these names.**

_____________________________________

_____________________________________

<hr>



*I am no longer a component in the system. I am*

*________________________. The ground is owned. The*

*perimeter is set. The Pattern has a name and named things lose their power in the*

*dark.*

**I am still here. That is a start.**

❖ ❖ ❖

Date of Entry:

---

Signature:

---

# A Final Word

The bells are ringing.

Not because the war is over. Not because the

cost has been repaid or the rooms have been

cleared. The bells are ringing because the

Witness is still at the console and the testimony

is entered into evidence and the ground —
finally, honestly, permanently — belongs to the
man standing on it.

You are not behind. You are not broken. You
are in the field, filing the report, refusing to
look away.

That is the whole job.

That is everything.

*I'm still here. That's a start.*

— The Witness | The Echoes Project | 2026

# About the Author

The Witness spent decades in the high-stakes world of systems, database structures, and project mobilization — operating as a bootson-the-ground field reporter and systems specialist across some of the most demanding environments in the EPC world. He has since applied those same mechanical principles to the complex architecture of human recovery.

Through The Echoes Project, he has built a four-book series that maps the full architecture of survival — from the original installation of the Pattern to the count that completes it. Each book is a room. Each room had a cost. Together they form *The*

*Witness Series* — the first complete field report on the cost of surviving narcissistic systems, child loss, and the long road back to owned ground.

*The Echoes of Time* — The valley. The architecture of the system and the first map of the Pattern's reach across a lifetime.

*Empty Chairs* — The river. A survivor's account of three losses, 177 no's, and the one man who spoke the language of the Dangerous Place.

*Vilomah* — The holy night. A technical manual for the 18.7 million — the parents standing against the natural order, in the silence where their children once stood.

*COST* — The Book of David. The fourth book bears the weight of them all. The 2 AM testimony that could only be written after the others were finished. The ledger. The count complete.

He does not write as a clinician. He writes as a Witness — from inside the system, filing the report, refusing to look away. The Echoes Project provides technical protocols for navigating survival: moving beyond the Role Exit of trauma into a functioning life built on owned ground.

For direct systems advisory and deeper field reports, visit *The Echoes Project* at thewitnessechoes.com

## Before the count began —

*Reservations, Apprehensions & Good Times*

There is a story that comes before this one.

Before the 1968 road. Before the 178. Before the Nightwatchman took his post.

There was a life being lived. Fully. Loudly. With reservations about what was coming, apprehensions about what had already arrived, and — against all odds — some genuinely good times.

Three names. Two centuries. One witness. But before any of that — there was a man who had no idea what was being built around him.

*Reservations, Apprehensions & Good Times* is the prequel to The Witness Series. The record before the record. Coming soon.

— The Witness

# If you made it this far —

You stayed.

That is not a small thing. This book asked something of you. It asked you to sit in the 2 AM room, to look at the count, to hold the names. You didn't have to do that. You chose to.

Thank you.

The carrying started February 25, 1968.

A four-year-old boy in Prairie County, Arkansas. Allen Keith Richards. My brother. The first name on the count. The one the language forgot before I even knew there was a language being built.

He has been carried every day since.

This is the fourth room. The Book of David. The one that could only be written after the others were finished — and the one that could only be read by someone willing to go all the way through.

You went all the way through.

The Witness Series is complete. Four books. Four rooms. One count. One true record.

*The Echoes of Time* — the valley — is where it started.

*Empty Chairs* — the river — is where the count began.

*Vilomah* — the holy night — is for the ones standing against the natural order.

*COST* — the Book of David — is what it cost to survive all three.

If any of these books found you at the right moment — tell someone. Not for me. For them.

You are not behind. You are not broken.

## I see you.

— The Witness | The Echoes Project | 2026

thewitnessechoes.com

echoesproject.substack.com